KALEIDOSCOPE

STARS

by
Roy A. Gallant

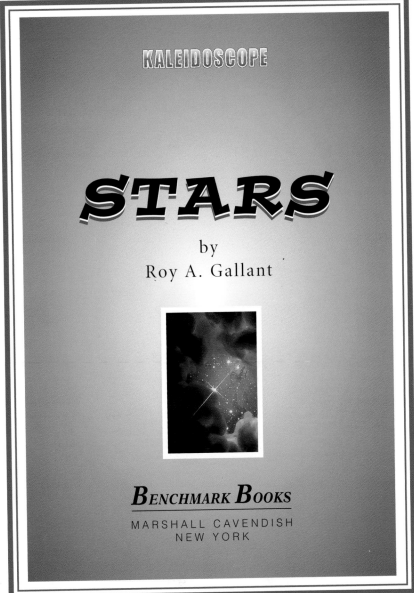

BENCHMARK BOOKS

MARSHALL CAVENDISH
NEW YORK

Series consultant:
Dr. Jerry LaSala, Chairman
Department of Physics
University of Southern Maine

Benchmark Books
Marshall Cavendish Corporation
99 White Plains Road
Tarrytown, New York 10591-9001

Library of Congress Cataloging-in-Publication Data
Gallant, Roy A.
Stars / by Roy A. Gallant
    p. cm. — (Kaleidoscope)
Includes bibliographical references and index.
Summary: Describes stars—how they are formed, their composition, and what happens when they die.
ISBN 0-7614-1036-8
1. Stars—Juvenile literature. [1. Stars.] I. Title. II. Kaleidoscope (Tarrytown, N.Y.)
QB801.7 G355 2001   523.8—dc21   99-047387

Photo research by Candlepants Incorporated

Cover photo: Photo Researchers/Seth Shostak/SPL

The photographs in this book are provided by permission and through the courtesy of:
Photo Researchers/ Frank Zullo: 5. Julian Baum/Science Photo Library: 6, 13, 21, 22, 29, 41. Royal Observatory, Edinburgh/SPL: 9. J. L. Charmet/SPL: 10. David A. Hardy/SPL: 14. Mount Stromlo and Siding Spring Observatories/SPL: 17. Space Telescope Science Institute/ NASA/SPL: 18, 26, 34. Joe Tucciarone/SPL: 25. Lynette Cook/SPL: 30. Celestial Image Co./SPL: 33, 42. CORBIS/Digital Art: 37. Photo Researchers/Mehau Kulyk/SPL: 38-39.

Printed in Italy

6 5 4 3 2 1

CONTENTS

A TRILLION LIGHTS

How many *stars* do you think there are in the night sky? How many can you see? Without a telescope, on a clear night you might be able to count more than 9,000 stars. With binoculars, you can see more than 50,000 stars, and even a small telescope brings thousands more into view. In total, countless trillions of stars are spread across the Universe. Some are red, while others are yellow or bluish white. If you stare at them long enough, you'll notice that the stars seem to twinkle. They don't really. The flickering you see is caused by Earth's shimmering air. The motion of the air causes the stars to look like they're blinking.

Starry, starry night.
This stargazer peers through his
telescope at the center of our Milky Way galaxy.

Can you name the star closest to Earth? It's the Sun. The Sun is our local star. It looks so much bigger than the other stars because it's right in our backyard. Because the Sun is so close, it's the easiest star to study, and so the one we know best. The Sun is 93 million miles (150 million kilometers) away. How far is that? If you sped there in a spaceship traveling 25,000 miles (40,230 kilometers) an hour, how long do you think it would take to reach the Sun—a day, a week, a month? It would take you a little over five months!

A fiery Sun shoots huge red tufts of gas off into space as the Ulysses *probe moves in for a closer look at the Sun's polar regions.*

The next nearest star is a smaller reddish one named Alpha Centauri. It is 270,000 times farther away than the Sun. To reach that star in our spaceship would take more than 100,000 years!

The Orion Nebula is a cloud of dust and gas lit up by many stars. It lies 1,500 light-years from Earth. A light-year is the distance light travels in one year. How long do you think it would take us to get there?

This time we would arrive in about 360 billion years. And our ship could keep going. There are stars that are even farther away!

Made up mostly of hydrogen, the Orion Nebula gives off a pinkish glow with a few patches of blue mixed in.

9

STAR PARTS

Ancient astronomers had no idea what the stars were made of. Some 3,000 years ago, people thought the stars were spirits that ruled over their lives. Still later, astronomers believed that stars were objects burning in the sky. Today we know that the stars do burn, just much hotter than a piece of wood or a lump of coal would.

Around the year 1000, Arabic astronomers started using an instrument called an astrolabe to measure the height of stars above the horizon.

Stars are gigantic balls of mostly *hydrogen* gas. The Sun, for instance, is so big that about 110 Earths could be lined up across its face. Like other stars, the Sun shines because the hydrogen deep down in its core, or center, is packed together and squeezed very tightly.

Gravity is the force that does the squeezing. It causes the hydrogen to heat up so much that its atoms *fuse*, or join, and become atoms of the gas helium. As a result of this change, the atoms send out light, heat, and all the other kinds of energy that reach Earth. In less than one second, the Sun gives off more energy than we have ever used on Earth. So, the Sun is the enormous energy factory that fuels our world.

Huge loops of hot gases, called prominences, blast out of the Sun from time to time. They can reach heights of hundreds of thousands of miles.

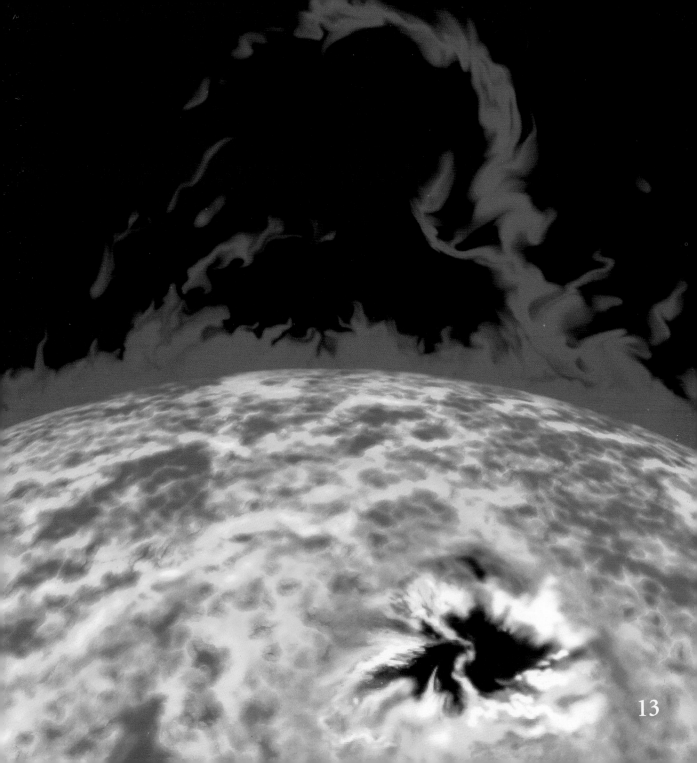

13

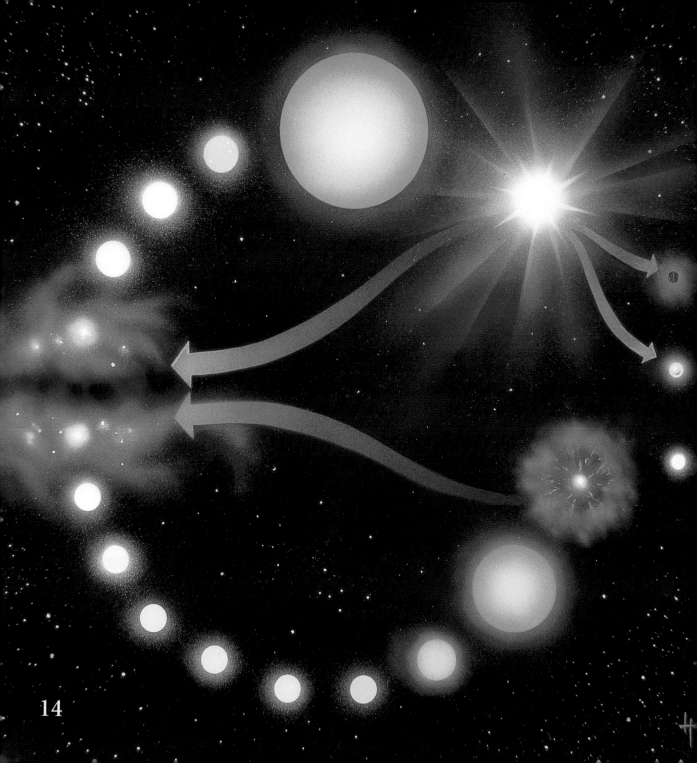

SEEING STARS

Stars are born, shine for several billion years, and then die. A star begins to die when it has used up all the hydrogen fuel in its core. People in ancient times believed that because the stars were spirits, they could create themselves out of nothing. Now we know that isn't true.

The life of two types of stars as they are born, grow old, and die. Stars like the Sun (bottom path) fade out as they shed their shell of gases. Even larger stars (top path) grow and grow, then end their lives in a huge explosion.

To witness the birth of a star, astronomers look in those mammoth clouds of gas and dust called *nebulae.* There are countless nebulae in space. Some are heavy and dark, others are as wispy as a feather, and many are very beautiful. Most are made of matter left over from the time the Universe began. Others are material cast off by aging or dying stars. Their cosmic dust is made up of tiny clumps of different kinds of atoms. The gases of the nebulae are mostly hydrogen with some helium mixed in.

Nebulae are the birthplace of stars. Gravity from the nebula's matter causes a cloud to pack itself around a central core. This heats the core and eventually makes the star shine.

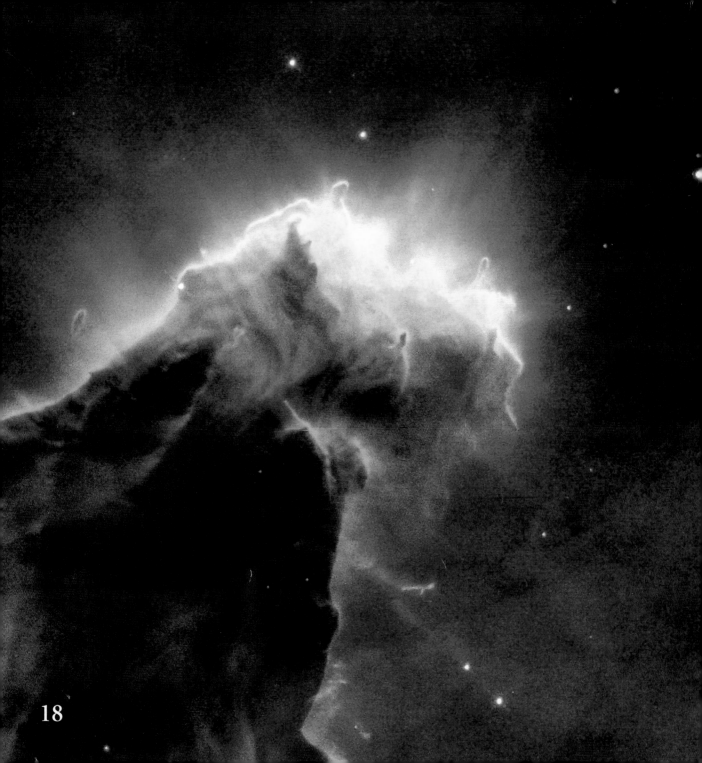

Here and there in a very thick nebula are dense globes of gas and dust. Called *globules*, these balls of gases draw in more matter, slowly growing bigger and bigger. Gravity packs this matter ever tighter around the globule's core. Over millions of years, the globule grows even larger by sweeping up smaller globules nearby.

The Eagle Nebula is a stellar nursery where stars are being born. The nebula is so large the entire Solar System could fit in a tiny patch of it.

Eventually the globule's matter is packed so tightly in the core that it begins to heat up and glow a fiery red. It is now called a *protostar*, or near star. Over millions of years more, the protostar grows even hotter and more massive until it becomes a full-grown star. Then it flashes on like a lightbulb. Its core has become hot enough to fuse hydrogen into helium and to send off vast amounts of energy.

After glowing a dull red, then a hot cherry red for thousands of years, a new star suddenly switches on its light.

21

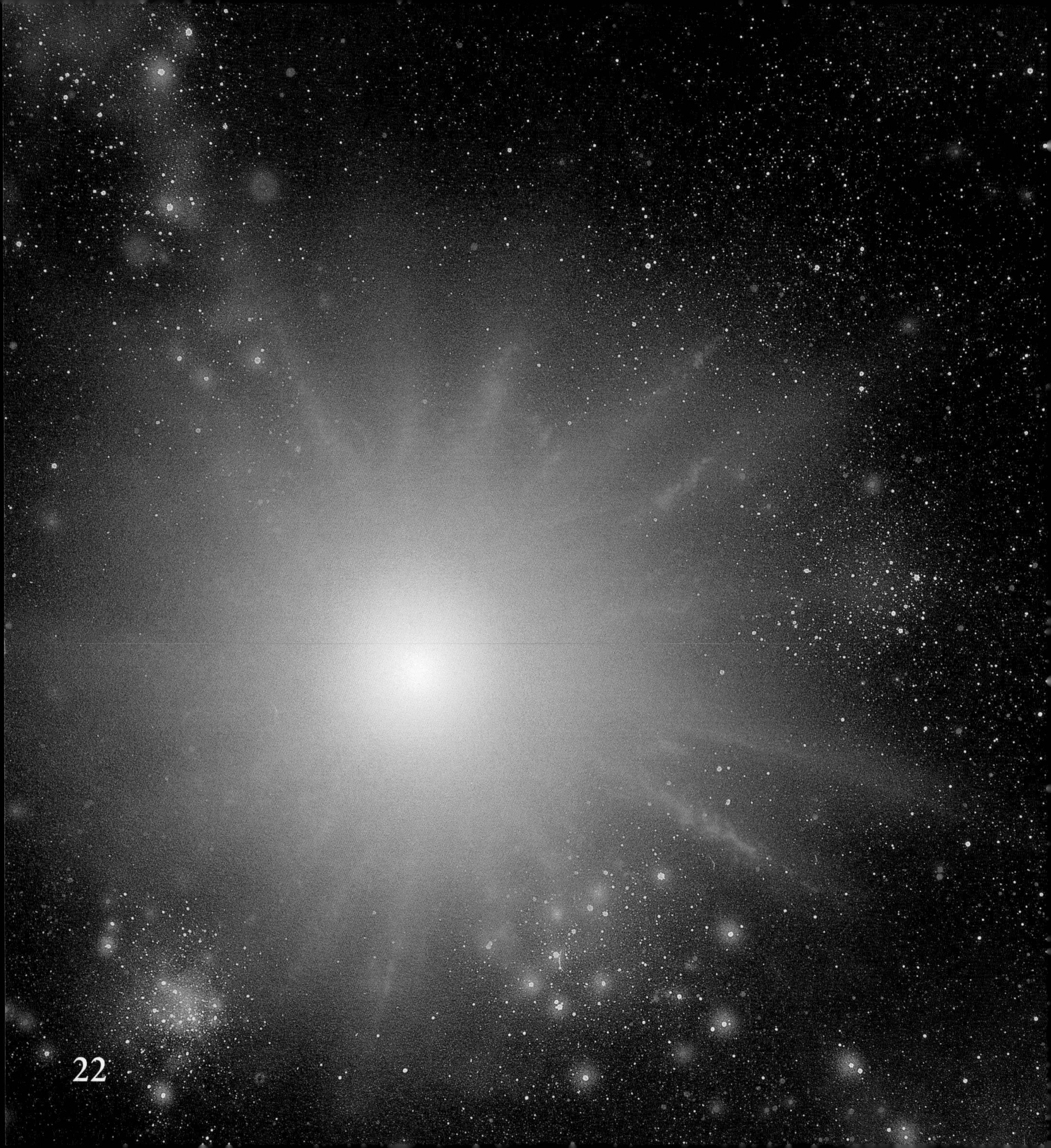

THE LIFE SPANS OF STARS

The kind of star that forms depends on the amount of matter a globule collects. Globules that capture the least amount of matter become stars called *red dwarfs*. They shine with a dull reddish light because their outer gas layers reach only a few thousand degrees. Since their core hydrogen burns slowly, their fuel lasts longer, and they live to be very old—perhaps a trillion years or more.

Here is a type of red dwarf known as a flare star. The surface gases of these unstable stars flare up, usually three or four times an hour.

23

Medium-mass stars like the Sun have more hydrogen than red dwarfs. But they burn a bit hotter and so use up their fuel faster. These stars shine with a yellowish light and live ten billion years or more before they begin to fade. The cores of the most massive stars, the blue giants and the blue *supergiants*, are raging infernos. Because they are so hot, they shine with a bluish white light and burn up their huge stores of hydrogen the fastest of all. The life span of a blue giant may be only tens of millions of years.

Wolf-Rayet stars, bluish white supergiants, are the hottest stars known. Some shine a million times brighter than the Sun.

26

RUNNING OUT OF GAS

When the fuel gauge of a red dwarf or a Sunlike star reaches "empty," the core begins to cool down. Then, the gases in the outer regions of the star come tumbling into the core. There is no longer enough pushing power in the core to hold the gases up, so gravity pulls them in.

This dying star casts off cloud after cloud of its surface gas. These gases balloon out and form a nebula. The dying star is the tiny white dot in the center.

When that happens, the gases bounce back off the core like a trampoline, and the dying star swells into a huge star called a *red giant*.

Over millions of years more, the red giant cools and slowly shrinks. As it does, the dying star's gases pack ever tighter together until the star is only a few times larger than planet Earth.

Billions of years in the future, as the Universe grows very old, most of the stars will be red giants. A red glow will fill the Universe.

29

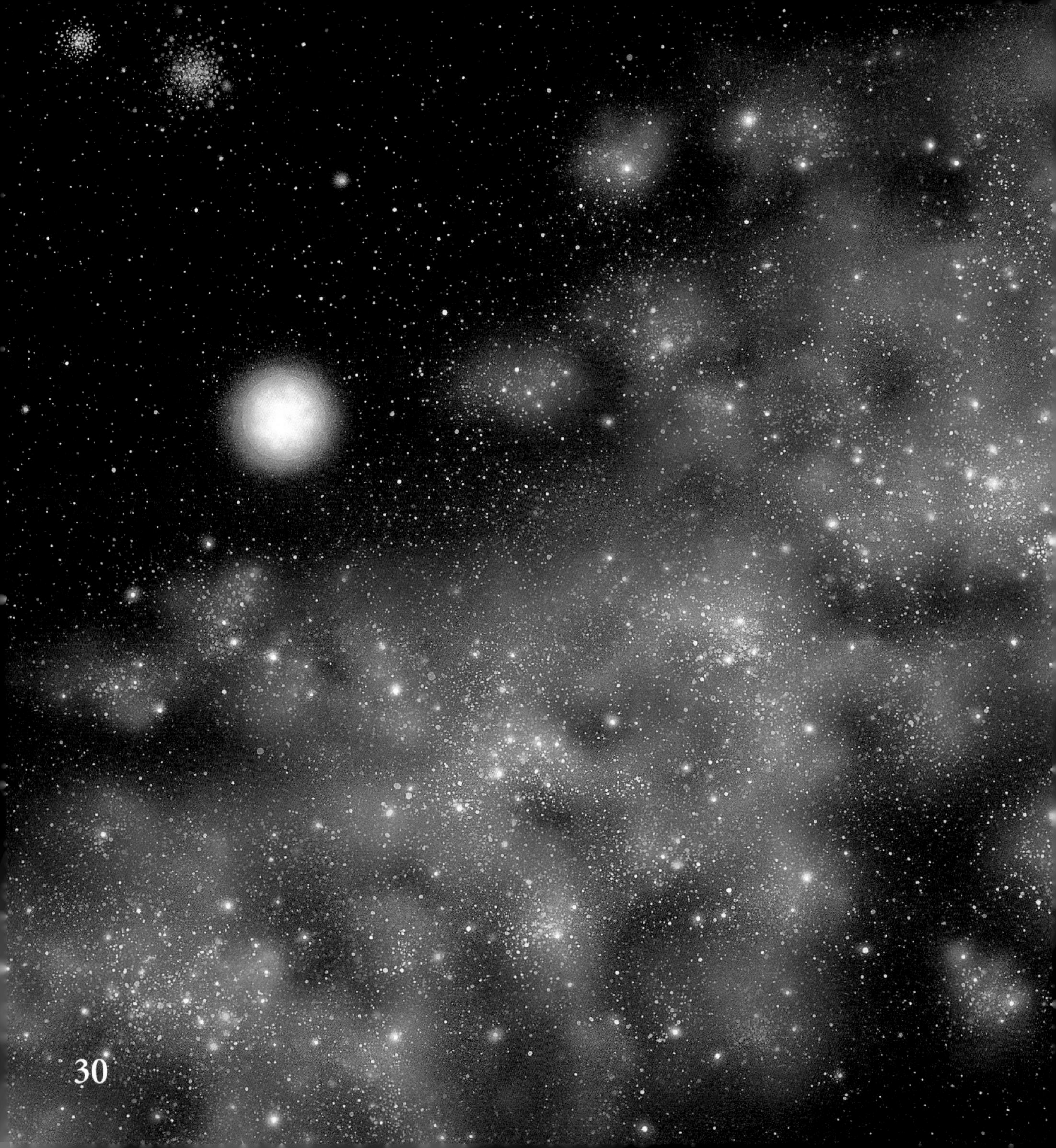

This packing action heats up the tiny star so much that it shines with a bright white light. Then the star finally shrinks down to about the size of Earth. It has become what astronomers call a *white dwarf.*

For perhaps billions of years more, the star cools and dims until it becomes a cold, dark object called a *black dwarf.* Has anyone ever seen a black dwarf? No, the Universe isn't old enough yet for a white dwarf to have faded into a black dwarf.

Against a background of young blue-white stars, a lone white dwarf shines out the last of its years.

A blue supergiant star ends its life in a very sudden and dramatic way. When its fuel is used up, the core cools so much that fusion can no longer take place. Then outer gases are pulled rapidly down into the core. In less than one-tenth of a second they explode, causing the star to blow itself to bits. The star has then become a *supernova*.

Here, a supernova has shot out most of its matter, leaving only the exposed core. Some of this matter can be seen as a veil of gases spreading through the constellation Vela.

33

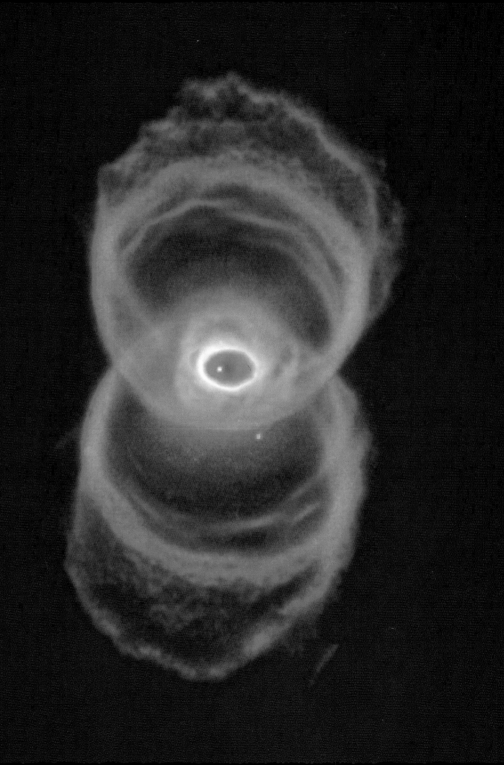

34

A supernova explosion is among the most violent events we have ever seen in the Universe. The explosion builds up atoms of many different chemical elements—gold, silver, lead, uranium, and others. Those atoms are then shot through space as a cloud of heavy elements.

All that is left of the supergiant is the exposed inner core, called a *neutron star*. This ball of extremely hot matter is only about 12 miles (20 kilometers) wide. Over billions of years the core will cool and dim until its light dies for good.

The beautiful Hourglass Nebula forms a double loop of gases sent out by a dying red giant. The red giant has become a white dwarf, which is the tiny white dot within the patch of blue.

BLACK HOLES

If a supernova star has about three times more matter than the Sun, then something even more interesting happens. It collapses so violently that the core simply disappears from view. It becomes a *black hole.*

Here is what we think happens when a black hole is formed: The core of the dead supernova has so much matter packed into such a small space that its gravity is superstrong. It is so powerful that nothing can escape it, not even light. If light can't escape from the object, there is no way to see it. So if we can't see it, how do we know it's there?

What do black holes look like?
How do they form? Most pictures of
black holes are left to the artist's imagination.

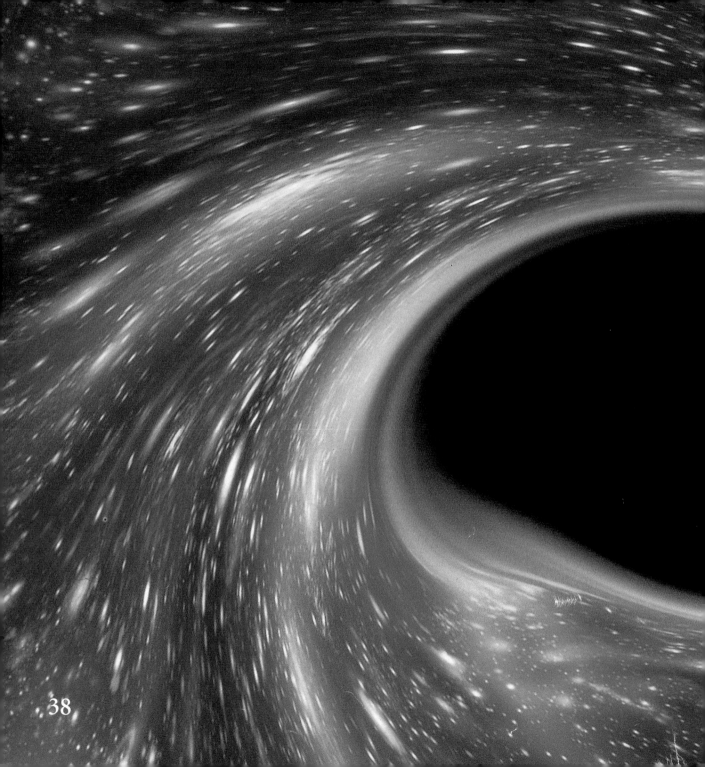

A computer's version of a black hole. Black holes are the extremely dense burned-out cores of supernova stars. They are so dense that no energy at all—not even light—can escape.

If a black hole happens to have a companion star nearby, then the black hole's intense gravity will pull off and gobble up some of the neighboring star's gases. As it does, it forms a whirling disk of gases spiraling around the black hole. We can detect those gases and know that a black hole is there.

A disk of gases circles a black hole. X-rays given off by these swirling gases are the only proof black holes exist.

41

WE COME FROM THE STARS

About five billion years ago, the Solar System was formed out of a nebula. That nebula was mostly hydrogen with a special kind of cosmic dust mixed in. The dust was part of a cloud produced by a supernova explosion. So the chemical elements that formed our planet billions of years ago were made in the heart of a supernova and then shot out into space. Since Earth and all its living things were formed out of that giant dust cloud, your body contains atoms of carbon, iron, and other elements created in that explosion. We, and all other life on Earth, come from the stars.

The nebula NGC 1977 is known as a reflection nebula. That means it doesn't give off its own light. Instead, its dust particles reflect the light of nearby stars.

GLOSSARY

Black dwarf   A star that has passed through the white-dwarf stage and is giving off so little energy that it can no longer be seen.

Black hole   An extremely massive star that has burned itself out. Black holes are so dense, and their gravity so strong, that nothing is able to escape from them, not even light.

Fuse   To join the nuclei of one element (hydrogen, for example) to form the nuclei of a heavier element (helium from hydrogen, for example).

Globule   An especially dense collection of gas and dust within a nebula that appears to be the first stage in star formation. Globules are observed in many nebulae.

Hydrogen   The simplest and lightest of all the chemical elements, and the most plentiful element in the Universe.

Nebula   A great cloud of gas and dust within a galaxy.

Neutron star   A star made up of those parts of an atom called neutrons. Neutrons add mass to an atom but lack an electric charge.

Protostar   A newly forming star that has not yet begun to give off energy.

Red dwarf   A star with little mass and a low surface temperature, which causes it to shine with a reddish light.

Red giant   An enormous star that shines with a reddish light because of its low surface temperature. Most stars go through a red-giant stage after they use up their core hydrogen. The star collapses and swells up as a red giant.

Star   A hot, glowing globe of gases that emits energy by fusing hydrogen into helium. The Sun is a typical star.

Supergiant   An extremely massive and hot star that shines with a bluish white light, gives off huge amounts of energy, and has a short life span.

Supernova   A giant star whose brightness is increased by a huge explosion when the star can no longer fuse elements and collapses in on itself.

White dwarf   A burned-out star that is very small and that gives off stored energy rather than new energy made through nuclear fusions. Sunlike stars end their lives as white dwarfs.

FIND OUT MORE

Books:

Bendick, Jeanne. *The Stars: Lights in the Night Sky.* Brookfield, CT: Millbrook, 1991.

Berger, Melvin and Gilda Berger. *Where Are the Stars during the Day? A Book about Stars.* Broomall, PA: Chelsea House, 1998.

Dexter, Robin. *Stars.* Mahwah, NJ: Troll, 1995.

Estalella, Robert. *The Stars.* Hauppauge, NY: Barron, 1993.

Fradin, Dennis B. *Space: Constellations.* Danbury, CT: Childrens Press, 1997.

Gustafson, John R. *Stars, Clusters, and Galaxies.* Parsippany, NJ: Silver Burdett, 1993.

Lambert, David. *Stars and Planets.* Austin: Raintree Steck-Vaugh, 1995.

Lurie, Alison. *Heavenly Zoo: Legends and Tales of the Stars.* New York: Farrar, Strauss & Giroux, 1996.

Moore, Patrick. *The Stars.* Brookfield, CT: Millbrook, 1993.

Packard, Mary. *Stars and Planets.* Mahwah, NJ: Troll, 1995.

Rosen, Sidney. *How Far Is a Star?* Minneapolis: Lerner, 1991.

Simon, Seymour. *Stars.* New York: Morrow, 1988.

Sipiera, Paul P. *Stars.* Danbury, CT: Childrens Press, 1997.

Websites:

The Web Nebulae
www.seds.org/billa/twn

Constellations
www.seds.org/Maps/Const/constS.html

Messier Deep-Sky Catalog
www.seds.org/messier

The Virtual Sun
sirius.astro.uva.nl/~michielb/sun/

Sun
www.hawastsoc.org/solar/eng/sun.html

The Sun
seds.lpl.arizona.edu/billa/tnp/sol.html

Virtual Trip to Black Holes and Neutron Stars
antwrp.gsfc.nasa.gov/htmltest/rjn_bht.html

Black Holes
www.uncg.edu/~aavolkov/bh/frames.html

AUTHOR'S BIO

Roy A. Gallant, called "one of the deans of American science writers for children" by *School Library Journal,* is the author of more than eighty books on scientific subjects. Since 1979, he has been director of the Southworth Planetarium at the University of Southern Maine, where he holds an adjunct full professorship. He lives in Rangeley, Maine.

INDEX

12/00